LAKE AND POND
FOOD WEBS

BY PAUL FLEISHER

LERNER PUBLICATIONS COMPANY • MINNEAPOLIS

The photographs in this book are used with the permission of: © Natalie Fobes/The Image Bank/Getty Images, p. 1; © Hisao Osono/Amana Images/Getty Images, p. 5; © Roy Toft/National Geographic/Getty Images, p. 6; © age fotostock/SuperStock, pp. 7, 20; © Tom Murphy/National Geographic/Getty Images, p. 8; © Gary Meszaros/Visuals Unlimited, pp. 9, 16, 25, 27, 46; © Wally Eberhart/Visuals Unlimited, p. 10; © BIOS Gilson François/Peter Arnold, Inc., p. 11; © H. Frei/Peter Arnold, Inc., p. 12; © Kevin Cullimore/Dorling Kindersley/Getty Images, p. 13; © Theo Allofs/Photonica/Getty Images, p. 14; © Doug Sokell/Visuals Unlimited, pp. 17, 41; © John Gerlach/Visuals Unlimited, p. 18; © George Grall/National Geographic/Getty Images, p. 19; © Jeff Foott/Discovery Channel Images/Getty Images, p. 21; © Ian Moar/OSF/Animals Animals, p. 22; © Wim van Egmond/Visuals Unlimited, p. 23; © Hans Pfletschinger/ Peter Arnold, Inc., p. 24; R. Town/U.S. Fish and Wildlife Service, p. 26; © Bill Beatty/Visuals Unlimited, p. 28; © Joe McDonald/Visuals Unlimited, pp. 29, 33; © Steve Maslowski/Visuals Unlimited, p. 30; © Bruce and Nancy Cushing/Visuals Unlimited, p. 31; © Ken Lucas/Visuals Unlimited, p. 32; © Charles Krebs/CORBIS, p. 34; © Glenn Oliver/Visuals Unlimited, p. 35; © Dr. Dennis Kunkel/Visuals Unlimited, p. 36; Eric Engbretson/U.S. Fish and Wildlife Service, p. 37; © Larry Mellichamp/Visuals Unlimited, p. 38; © First Light/Getty Images, p. 39; © Paul Damien/National Geographic/Getty Images, p. 40; © Kirtley-Perkins/Visuals Unlimited, p. 42; © Bill Curtsinger/National Geographic/Getty Images, p. 43; PhotoDisc Royalty Free by Getty Images, p. 47; © Inge Ekstrom/Nordic Photos/Getty Images, p. 48 (top); © John G. Shedd Aquarium/Visuals Unlimited, p. 48 (bottom). Illustrations on pp. 4, 15 by Zeke Smith, © Lerner Publishing Group, Inc.

Cover: © Jeff Foott/Discovery Channel Images/Getty Images (top); © iStockphoto.com/Johnny Lye (bottom left); © Getty Images (bottom right); © Natalie Fobes/The Image Bank/Getty Images (background).

Lerner Publications Company
A division of Lerner Publishing Group, Inc.
241 First Avenue North
Minneapolis, MN 55401 U.S.A

Website address: www.lernerbooks.com

Library of Congress Cataloging-in-Publication Data

Fleisher, Paul.
  Lake and pond food webs / by Paul Fleisher.
      p.   cm. — (Early bird food webs)
   Includes index.
   ISBN: 978-0-8225-6731-8 (lib. bdg. : alk. paper) 1. Lake
ecology—Juvenile literature. 2. Pond ecology—Juvenile
literature. 3. Food chains (Ecology)—Juvenile literature. I. Title
QH541.5.L3F58 2008
577.63—dc22   2007001372

Manufactured in the United States of America
1 2 3 4 5 6 – JR – 13 12 11 10 09 08

CONTENTS

Be A Word Detective 5

Chapter 1
LAKES AND PONDS 6

Chapter 2
LAKE AND POND PLANTS 14

Chapter 3
LAKE AND POND PLANT EATERS 22

Chapter 4
LAKE AND POND MEAT EATERS 27

Chapter 5
LAKE AND POND DECOMPOSERS 34

Chapter 6
PEOPLE AND LAKES 39

A Note to Adults on Sharing a Book 44

Learn More about Lakes, Ponds, and Food Webs . . . 45

Glossary 46

Index 48

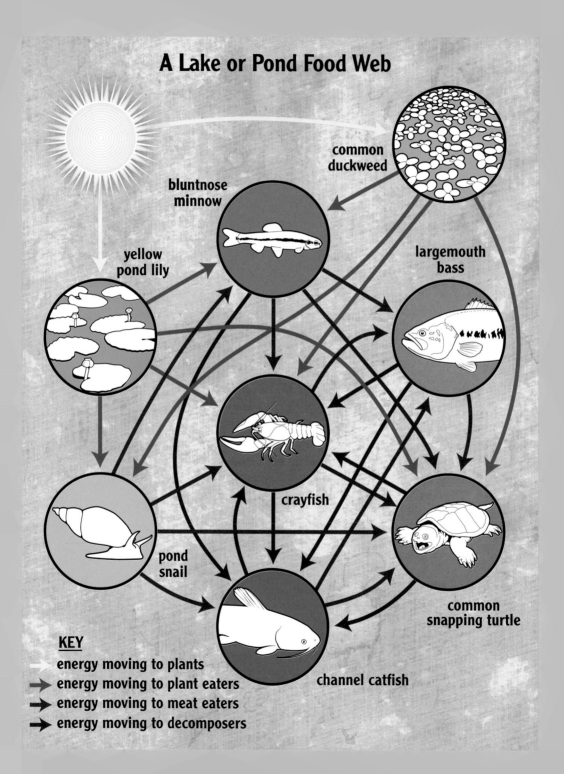

A Lake or Pond Food Web

common duckweed

bluntnose minnow

yellow pond lily

largemouth bass

crayfish

pond snail

common snapping turtle

channel catfish

KEY
- energy moving to plants
- energy moving to plant eaters
- energy moving to meat eaters
- energy moving to decomposers

BE A WORD DETECTIVE

Can you find these words as you read about lake and pond food webs? Be a detective and try to figure out what they mean. You can turn to the glossary on page 46 for help.

algae	environment	oxygen
bacteria	food chain	photosynthesis
carnivores	food web	producers
consumers	herbivores	scavengers
decay	nutrients	
decomposers	omnivores	

This bird is a great blue heron. It has caught a fish. Where do herons hunt for food?

CHAPTER 1
LAKES AND PONDS

A tall bird wades in a lake. The bird is a great blue heron. The heron stands very still. Then it stabs its beak into the water. It catches a fish.

Herons hunt in the shallow water of lakes and ponds. Many creatures live in the water. Others live along the water's edge. Plants grow in the water too. Insects fly above it. Frogs hop along the shore. Birds and other animals come here to drink and to hunt for food.

A young white-tailed deer has come to a pond to drink water.

Lakes and ponds are some of Earth's most important environments. An environment is the place where any creature lives. The environment includes the air, soil, and weather. It includes plants and animals too.

Ducks tip over to eat underwater plants.

Many fish eat meat. This bass is eating a frog.

Plants and animals in lakes and ponds depend on one another. Some animals eat plants. Other animals are meat eaters. They eat other animals. When plants and animals die, they decay. They break down into chemicals (KEH-muh-kuhlz). Some of the chemicals are called nutrients (NOO-tree-uhnts). Living things need nutrients to grow.

Energy moves from one living thing to another. A food chain shows how the energy moves. The energy for life comes from the sun. Plants store the sun's energy in their leaves, stems, and roots. When an animal eats a plant, the animal gets some of the sun's energy from the plant. The energy moves farther along the food chain each time one living thing eats another.

A fish is watching a frog. If the fish eats the frog, the fish will get energy from the frog.

A tadpole is a young frog. This tadpole is eating a plant.

Lakes have many food chains. Imagine that a tadpole eats a plant. Then a sunfish eats the tadpole. A heron eats the sunfish. When the heron dies, a crayfish eats its body. The sun's energy goes from the plant to the tadpole. Then it passes to the sunfish. Then it goes to the heron. Then it goes to the crayfish.

But sunfish don't eat only tadpoles. They eat insects and minnows too. Herons eat many different kinds of fish. And crayfish eat many kinds of living and dead animals.

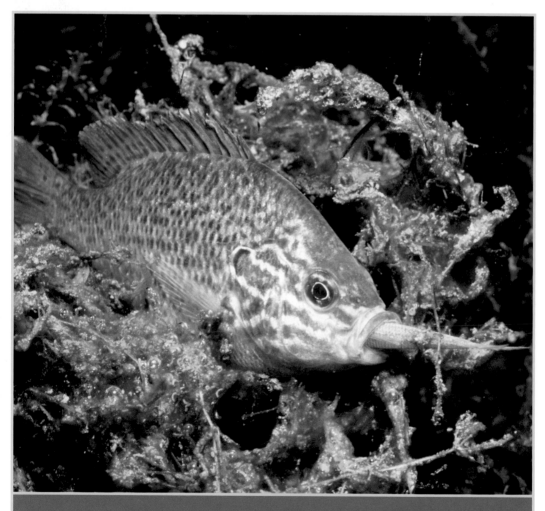

This sunfish is eating a smaller fish.

The plants and animals that live in lakes depend on each other.

An environment's food web is made up of many food chains. A food web shows how all living things depend on one another for food.

Water lilies are green plants that grow in lakes and ponds. How do green plants use sunlight?

CHAPTER 2
LAKE AND POND PLANTS

Green plants use sunlight to make food.
Because plants produce food, they are called
producers. Plants also make oxygen (AHK-sih-
juhn). Oxygen is a gas in the air. All animals
need oxygen to breathe.

The way plants make food and oxygen is
called photosynthesis (FOH-toh-SIHN-thuh-sihs).
Plants need carbon dioxide, sunlight, and water

for photosynthesis. Carbon dioxide is a gas in the air. A plant's leaves take in carbon dioxide and sunlight. The plant's roots take in water. The plant uses energy from sunlight to turn the carbon dioxide and water into sugar and starch. Sugar and starch are the plant's own food. The plant stores this food in its leaves and roots.

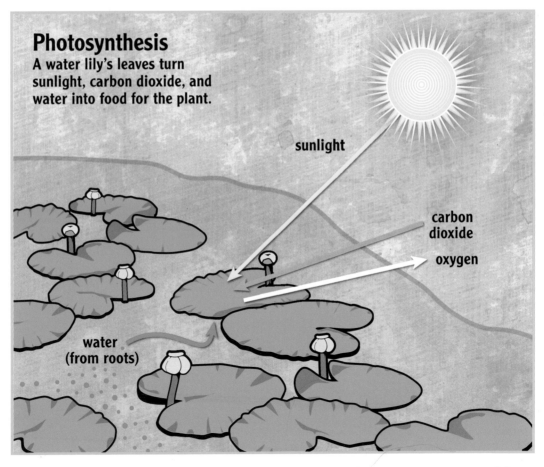

Photosynthesis
A water lily's leaves turn sunlight, carbon dioxide, and water into food for the plant.

sunlight

carbon dioxide

oxygen

water (from roots)

This is a young red-spotted newt. It has gills behind its eyes. The newt uses its gills to breathe oxygen that is in the water.

As the plant makes food, it also makes oxygen. The oxygen goes into the air and the water. Animals breathe in the oxygen. They breathe out carbon dioxide. Plants use the carbon dioxide to make more food.

Algae (AL-jee) are tiny plants. They float in the water. Algae are the most important producers in the pond. But most algae are so small we can't see them.

Sometimes algae piles up in thick mats. You can see bubbles of oxygen in this algae mat. The algae made the oxygen through photosynthesis.

Many green duckweed plants are floating in this lake. The duckweed plants are tiny compared to the maple tree leaf.

Larger plants live in lakes too. Duckweed plants float on top of the water. They have short roots. The roots hang in the water. They do not grow down into the soil at the bottom of the lake.

The roots of water lilies reach down through the water. They grow into the mud at the bottom. Water lilies have light, spongy leaves. Their leaves float on the water's surface.

Water lilies grow from the pond's bottom to the top of the water.

Other plants grow in shallow water along the shore. Their roots grow in the mud at the bottom of the pond. Wild rice is a kind of grass. It grows in shallow water. Cattails grow at the edge of the pond too.

Cattail flowers look a bit like the tail of a brown cat. Seeds grow in the flowers.

This lake is in a place that has cold winters. The top of the water has frozen into ice. But plants and animals are still living under the ice.

Some plants die each fall, when the weather gets colder. But before they die, they make seeds. The next spring, new plants grow from the seeds.

Other plants turn brown in the fall, but they don't die. Their roots live through the winter. Their seeds live too. In the spring, new leaves grow from the plants' roots. And new plants grow from the seeds.

Pond snails eat algae and other kinds of plants. What are some other plant-eating animals that live in lakes and ponds?

CHAPTER 3
LAKE AND POND PLANT EATERS

Animals are called consumers. *Consume* means "eat." Animals that eat only plants are called herbivores (ER-buh-vorz). Energy from the sun is stored inside plants. When an animal eats a plant, it gets the sun's energy.

Some herbivores are tiny. Look at a jar full of pond water. You can see hundreds of tiny specks. The specks are swimming. Each one is a little animal. Copepods (KOH-puh-pahdz) and daphnia (DAF-nee-uh) are tiny animals that look like shrimp. Copepods and daphnia eat algae.

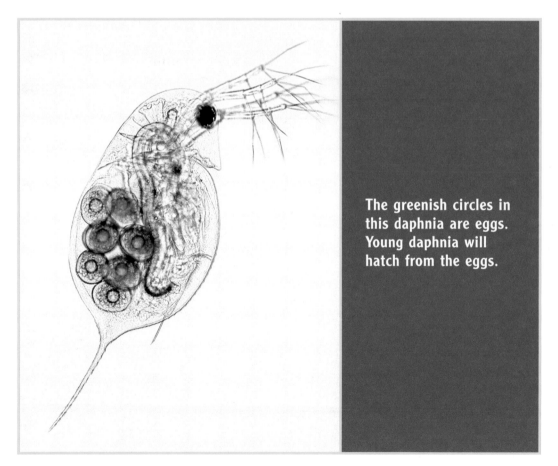

The greenish circles in this daphnia are eggs. Young daphnia will hatch from the eggs.

Young mayflies have gills on their backs for breathing underwater.

Many insects live in or near water.
Mayflies live near lakes and ponds. They lay
their eggs in the water. Baby insects hatch out
of the eggs. They live in the water. The young
mayflies eat algae.

Larger animals also eat lake plants. Snails
have rough tongues. They use their tongues to
scrape algae off of rocks.

Some fish are herbivores. Shiners and minnows eat plants. Carp grow large by eating underwater plants.

Some birds are herbivores too. Mallard ducks and Canada geese eat plants. In the fall, some lake plants produce seeds. Many birds feast on the seeds.

Some carp are very big. They can be longer than a yardstick.

Other animals are herbivores too. Muskrats and beavers live in lakes and ponds. Muskrats eat roots, seeds, stems, and leaves. Beavers eat twigs and bark. Deer come to lakes to drink water. They eat plants growing along the shore.

This animal is a muskrat. Muskrats are good swimmers.

Many fish eat meat. What do we call animals that eat meat?

CHAPTER 4
LAKE AND POND MEAT EATERS

Some lake and pond creatures eat meat. These animals are called carnivores (KAHR-nuh-vorz). Carnivores eat animals. But they need plants too. Carnivores get energy by eating animals that have eaten plants.

Many insects are carnivores. Dragonflies fly above lakes and ponds. They hunt mosquitoes and other flying insects. Young dragonflies live in the water. They eat insects too.

This dragonfly has caught a mosquito.

Water snakes are good swimmers. They eat fish, frogs, and tadpoles.

Frogs are carnivores. They catch insects and other small animals. Water snakes swim through the water. They hunt for fish and frogs.

Many fish are carnivores. Bass eat smaller fish. They also eat insects and frogs.

Many kinds of birds live near lakes and ponds. Kingfishers perch on branches near the water. Then they dive into the water. They catch small fish in their beaks.

Kingfishers eat mostly fish. But they also hunt crayfish, snails, and other small animals.

At night, bats fly close to the water to catch fish.

At night, bats fly over lakes and ponds. They catch and eat flying insects. Some bats can even catch small fish swimming in the water.

Some animals are omnivores. Omnivores are animals that eat both plants and animals. Catfish are omnivores. They swim at the bottom of lakes and ponds. Catfish eat plants. They hunt for fish, insects, and worms. They also eat animals that have died and fallen to the bottom.

Catfish eat mostly meat. But they also eat underwater plants, algae, and seeds that fall into the water.

This raccoon is eating a fish.

Raccoons are also omnivores. Raccoons often live near lakes and ponds. They look for food in and near the water. Raccoons eat fruit and berries. They also eat frogs, snakes, crayfish, and bird eggs.

Dead leaves and pine needles have fallen into this pond. What will happen to them?

CHAPTER 5

LAKE AND POND DECOMPOSERS

All living things die. When plants and animals die, they decay. They break down into nutrients. Living things called decomposers help dead things decay. Decomposers feed on dead plants

Decomposers are nature's recycling crew. Dead plants and animals sink to the bottom of the pond. Decomposers feed on them. Nutrients from the dead plants and animals become part of the mud on the bottom. The nutrients go back into the pond. Then other living things can use the nutrients.

This dead mosquito is covered with mold. The mold is breaking down the mosquito's body.

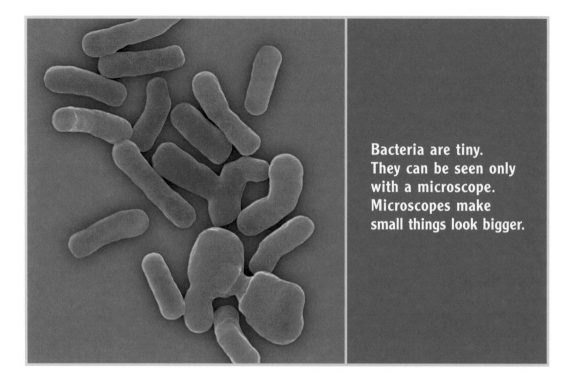

Bacteria are tiny.
They can be seen only
with a microscope.
Microscopes make
small things look bigger.

Decomposers are very important. Without them, lakes and ponds would become filled with dead plants and animals. Then no new plants could grow. Animals would run out of food.

Bacteria (bak-TEER-ee-uh) are the most important decomposers in lakes and ponds. Bacteria are too tiny for us to see. Millions of bacteria live in the water. Millions more live in the mud at the bottom.

Some animals eat plants and animals that have died. These animals are called scavengers (SKAV-uhn-juhrz). Catfish are scavengers. Crayfish are scavengers too.

Crayfish look like small lobsters.

Each year, plants die and fall into the water. Decomposers turn the dead plants into mud. Ponds and lakes slowly fill with mud. The water gets shallower. After many, many years, lakes and ponds may become dry land.

This wetland is a bog. It formed when moss grew on a lake's surface. After many years, the bog may become dry land.

Many people like to go boating on lakes. What are some other ways people use lakes?

CHAPTER 6
PEOPLE AND LAKES

Many people like to visit ponds and lakes. People go fishing and boating. They swim in the water on hot summer days.

People build towns and cities near lakes. Lakes have lots of water. People need water to drink and to wash with. They pump water from the lake. They add chemicals to the water to make sure it's clean. Then they pump it through pipes to people's homes.

Some lakes are very big. Ships travel on big lakes. The ships carry food, coal, and building supplies from city to city.

Lake Michigan is one of the biggest lakes in the United States. Huge ships travel on Lake Michigan. This ship is unloading coal.

Too much algae is growing in this pond.

Plants and animals that live in lakes need nutrients to grow. But sometimes lakes get too many nutrients. People put fertilizer on lawns or farms. Rain can wash fertilizer into lakes. Fertilizer has nutrients that plants need. It makes lawns green. It helps farm crops grow. But fertilizer makes algae grow too fast.

When too much algae grows in a lake, the water becomes cloudy. Underwater plants can't get enough light to grow. When the extra algae dies, bacteria break it down. Many kinds of bacteria use oxygen when they break down dead plants. As the bacteria break down the algae, they use most of the oxygen in the water. Fish in the lake may not have enough oxygen to breathe. The fish may die.

This lake doesn't have enough oxygen for fish to breathe. Many fish have died.

This snapping turtle lives in a lake in Florida.

Lakes and ponds are important. We must take care of them. If we don't, the water won't be good to drink. It won't be clean enough to swim in. It won't be a good home for plants and animals. People must treat ponds and lakes with care.

ON SHARING A BOOK

When you share a book with a child, you show that reading is important. To get the most out of the experience, read in a comfortable, quiet place. Turn off the television and limit other distractions, such as telephone calls. Be prepared to start slowly. Take turns reading parts of this book. Stop occasionally and discuss what you're reading. Talk about the photographs. If the child begins to lose interest, stop reading. When you pick up the book again, revisit the parts you have already read.

BE A VOCABULARY DETECTIVE

The word list on page 5 contains words that are important in understanding the topic of this book. Be word detectives and search for the words as you read the book together. Talk about what the words mean and how they are used in the sentence. Do any of these words have more than one meaning? You will find the words defined in a glossary on page 46.

WHAT ABOUT QUESTIONS?

Use questions to make sure the child understands the information in this book. Here are some suggestions:

> What did this paragraph tell us? What does this picture show? What is a food web? How do plants depend on animals? Where does a lake's energy come from? What do we call animals that eat both plants and animals? What happens if too much algae grows in a lake? What is your favorite part of the book? Why?

If the child has questions, don't hesitate to respond with questions of your own, such as What do *you* think? Why? What is it that you don't know? If the child can't remember certain facts, turn to the index.

INTRODUCING THE INDEX

The index helps readers find information without searching through the whole book. Turn to the index on page 48. Choose an entry such as *plants*, and ask the child to use the index to find out how plants make their own food. Repeat with as many entries as you like. Ask the child to point out the differences between an index and a glossary. (The index helps readers find information, while the glossary tells readers what words mean.)

LEARN MORE ABOUT
LAKES, PONDS, AND FOOD WEBS

BOOKS
Capeci, Anne. *Food Chain Frenzy.* New York: Scholastic, 2003.

Johnson, Rebecca L. *A Journey into a Lake.* Minneapolis: Lerner Publications Company, 2004.

Morrison, Gordon. *Pond.* Boston: Houghton Mifflin, 2002.

Riley, Peter. *Food Chains.* New York: Franklin Watts, 1998.

WEBSITES
Chain Reaction
http://www.ecokids.ca/pub/eco_info/topics/frogs/chain_reaction/index.cfm#
Create a food chain, and find out what happens if one link is taken out of the chain.

Lakes Are Great
http://www.dnr.state.wi.us/org/caer/ce/eek/nature/habitat/lakes.htm
Learn about lake wildlife, and find out how to get a good view of underwater plants and animals.

Ponds and Lakes
http://www.mbgnet.net/fresh/lakes/index.htm
Find out which lakes are the largest in the world, see pictures of the Great Lakes from space, and learn how lakes and ponds change over time.

Pond Life Animal Printouts
http://www.enchantedlearning.com/biomes/pond/pondlife.shtml
This page has links to information about many kinds of animals that live in and around lakes and ponds.

Something Froggy
http://fi.edu/fellows/fellow9/jun99/p-page_one.shtml
Learn all about frogs, and then play games about frogs.

GLOSSARY

algae (AL-jee): simple plants that have no leaves, stems, or roots. Algae grow in water or on wet surfaces.

bacteria (bak-TEER-ee-uh): tiny living things that are made up of just one cell. Bacteria can be seen only under a microscope.

carnivores (KAHR-nuh-vorz): animals that eat meat

consumers: living things that eat other living things. Animals are consumers.

decay: to break down

decomposers: living things that feed on dead plants and animals

environment: the place where any creature lives. An environment includes the air, soil, weather, plants, and animals in a place.

food chain: the way energy moves from the sun to a plant, then to a plant eater, then to a meat eater, and finally to a decomposer

food web: many food chains connected together. A food web shows how all living things in a place need one another for food.

herbivores (ER-buh-vorz): animals that eat only plants

nutrients (NOO-tree-uhnts): chemicals that living things need in order to grow

omnivores: animals that eat both plants and meat

oxygen (AHK-sih-juhn): a gas in the air. All animals need oxygen to breathe.

photosynthesis (FOH-toh-SIHN-thuh-sihs): the way green plants use energy from sunlight to make their own food out of carbon dioxide and water

producers: living things that make their own food. Plants are producers.

scavengers (SKAV-uhn-juhrz): animals that eat dead plants and animals

INDEX

Pages listed in **bold** type refer to photographs.

algae, 17, 23, 24, 41–42

breathing underwater, **16**, **24**

decomposers, 34–38

energy moving through a lake, 10

food chains and food webs, **4**, 10–13

meat eaters, 6–7, 9, **10**, **12**, 27–31, **32**, **33**

omnivores, 32–33

people and lakes, 39–41, 43
plant eaters, **8**, 9, **11**, 22–26
plants, 9, 14–21

scavengers, 37